Teen Coloring Book

This Coloring book for girls belongs to:

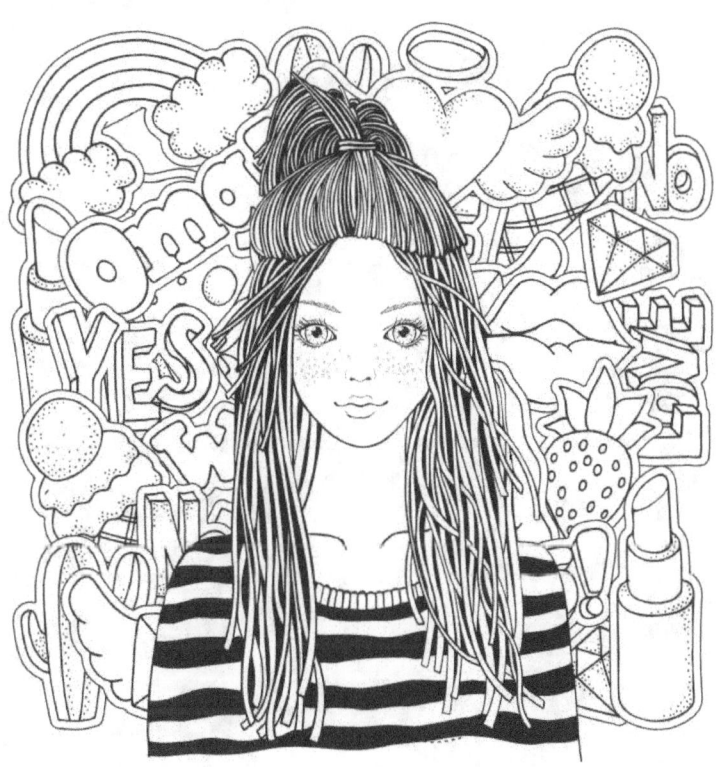

Copyright © 2019 Teen Coloring Books

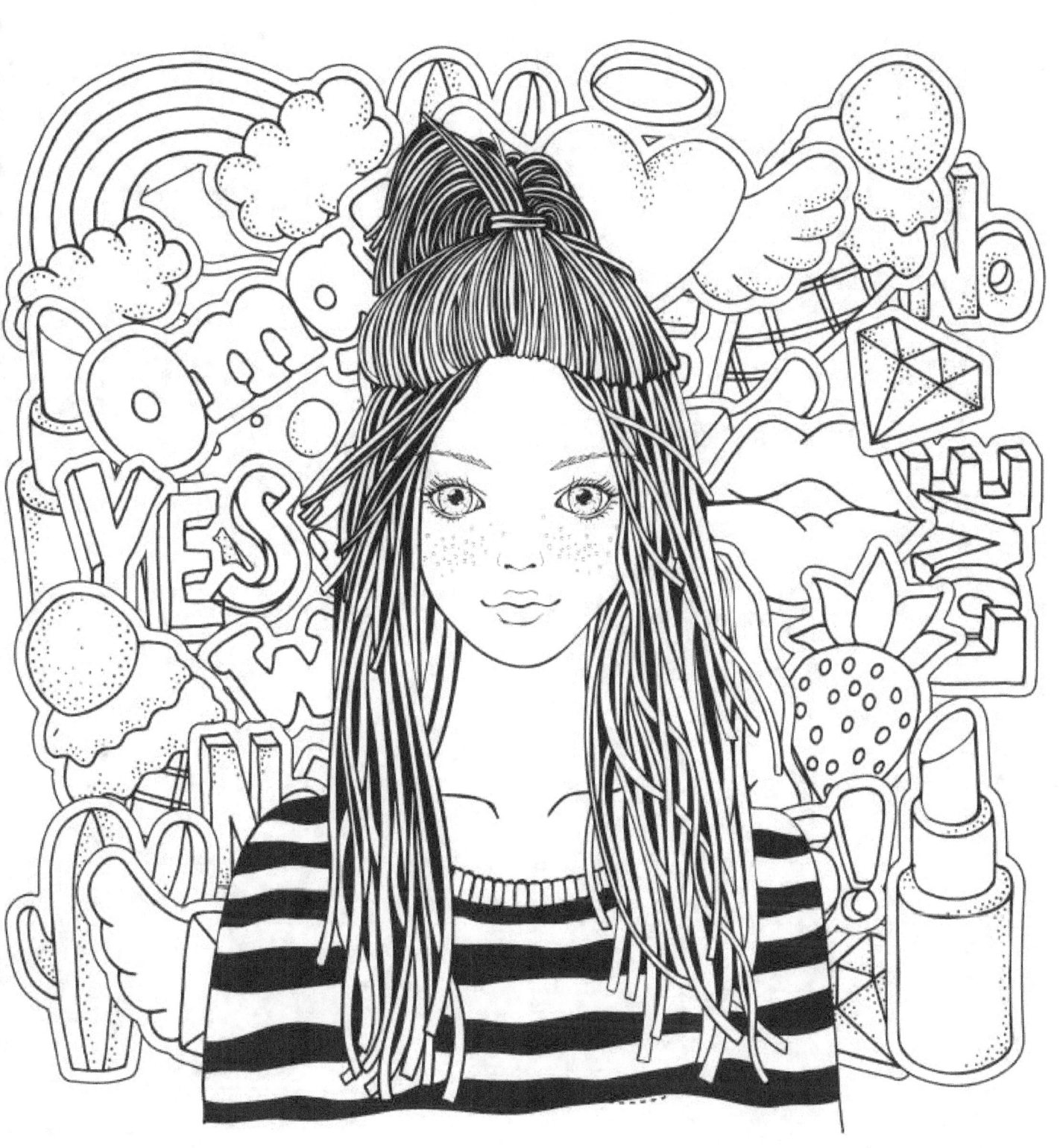

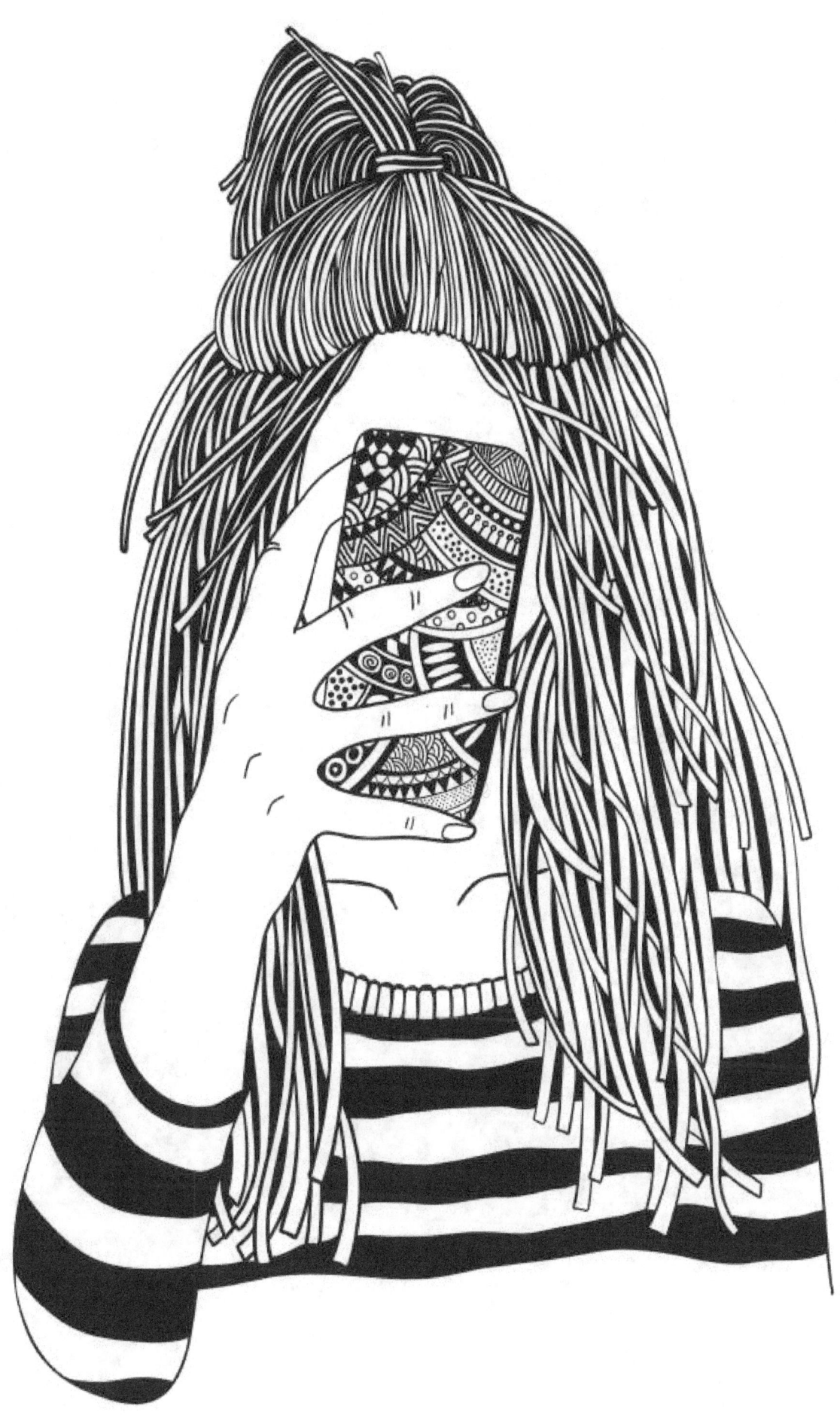

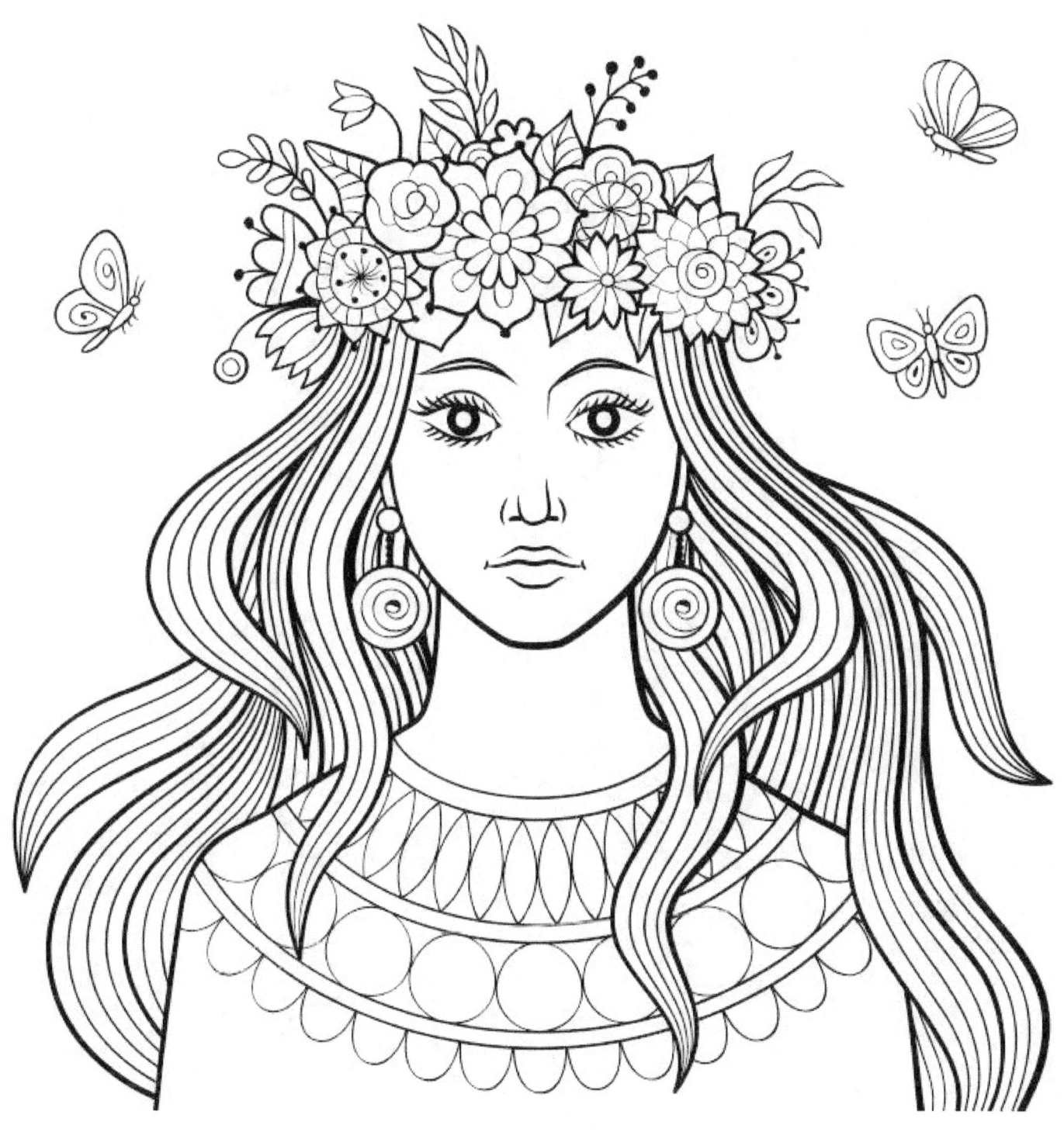

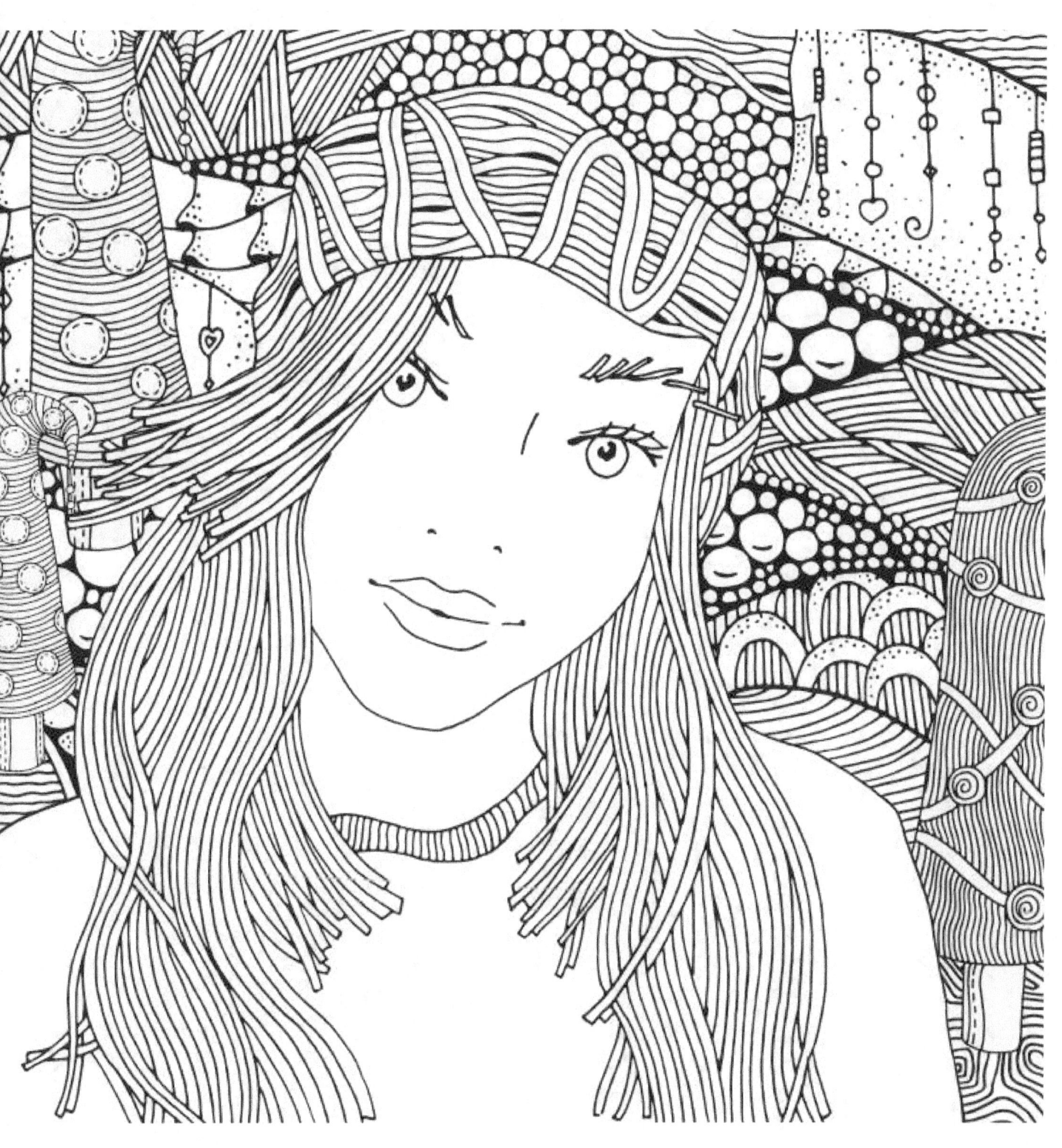

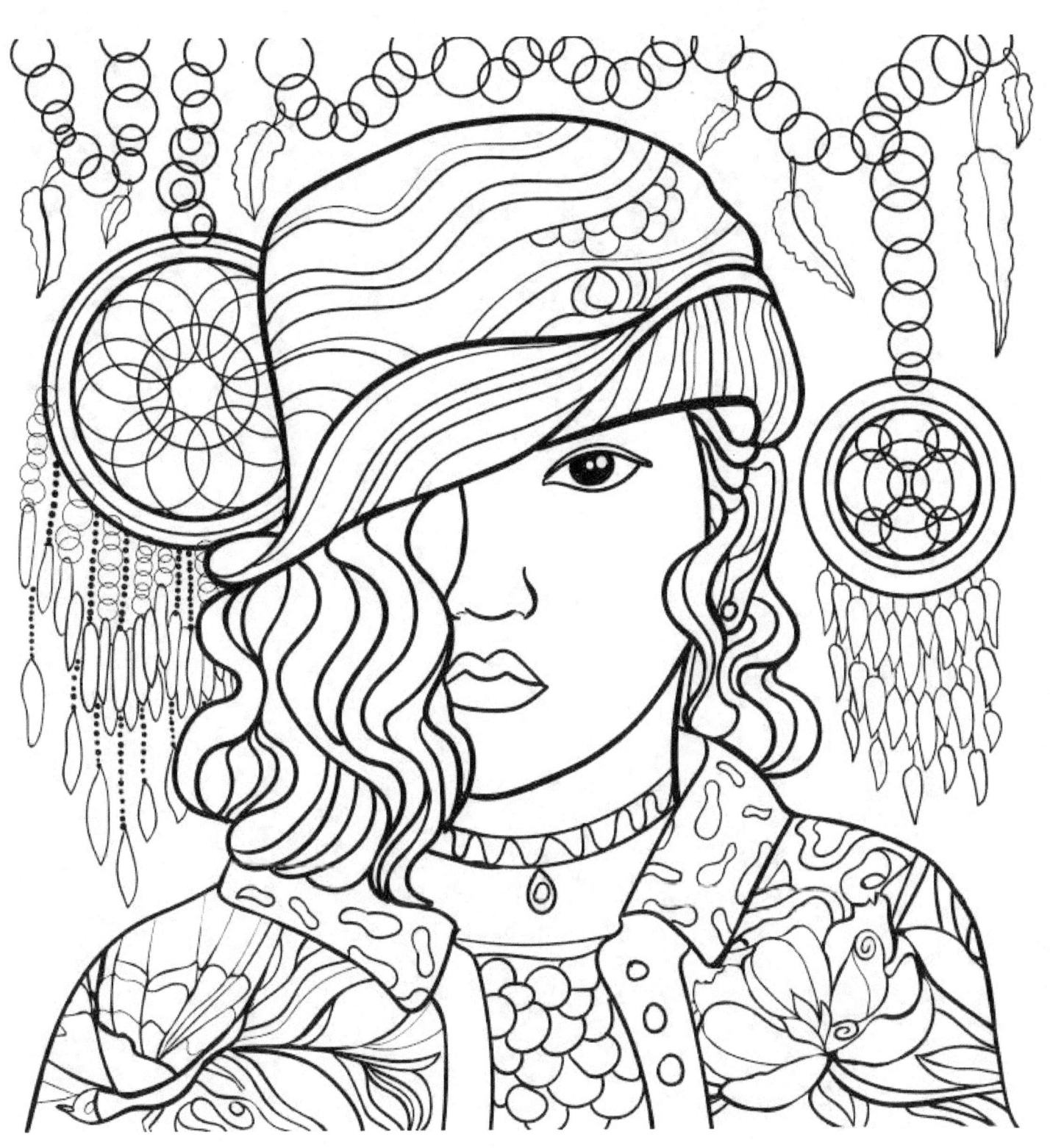

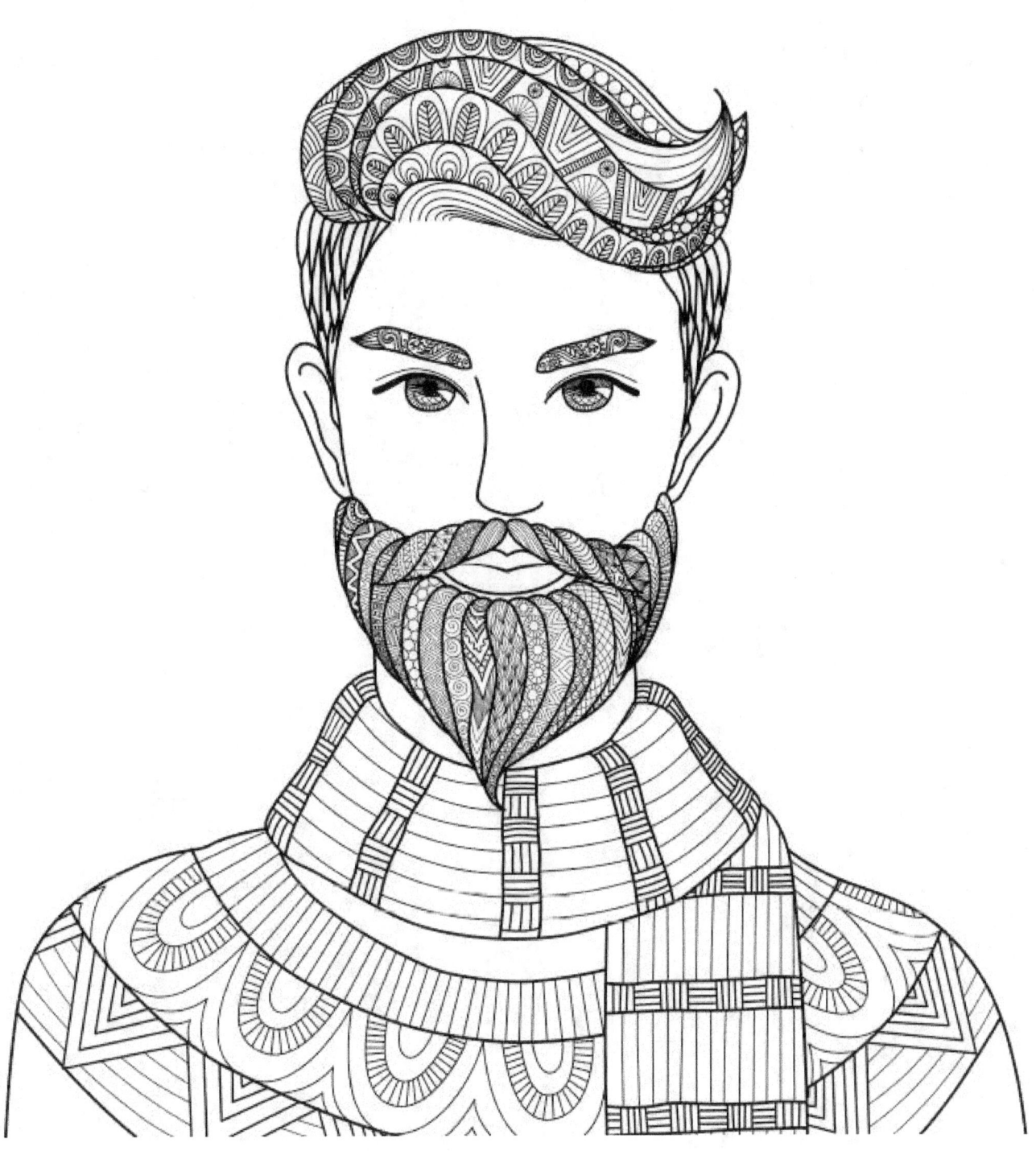

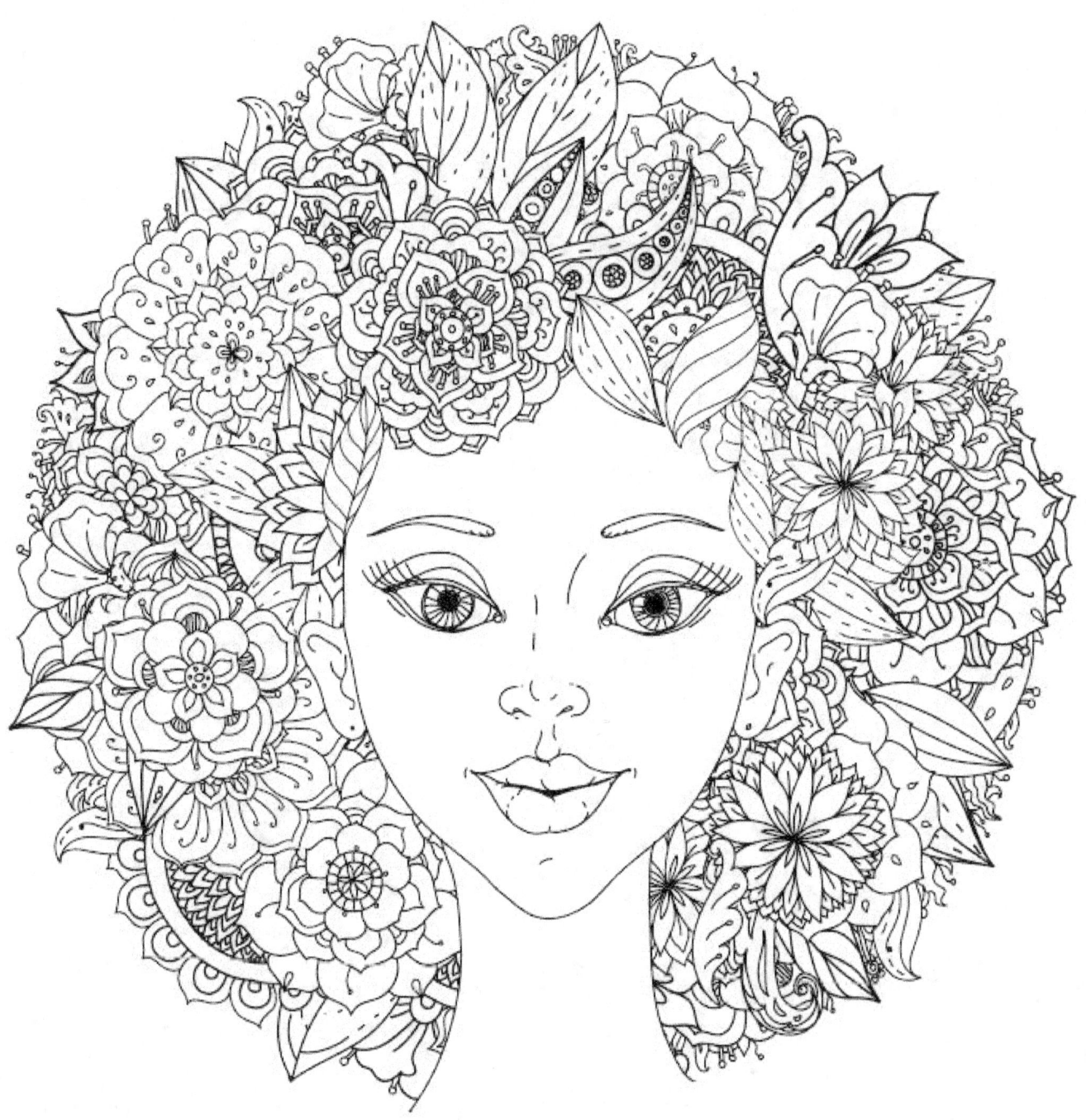

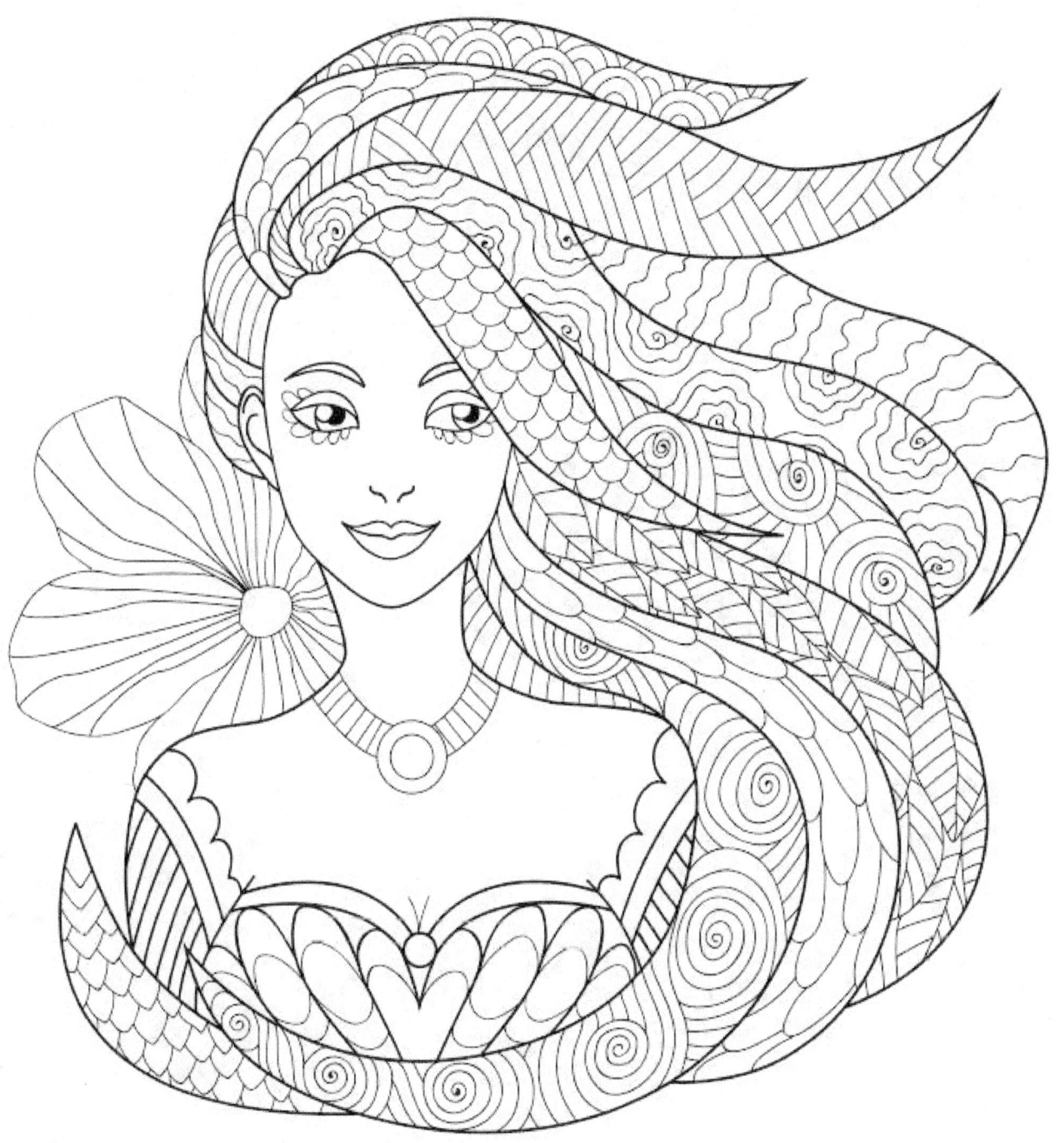

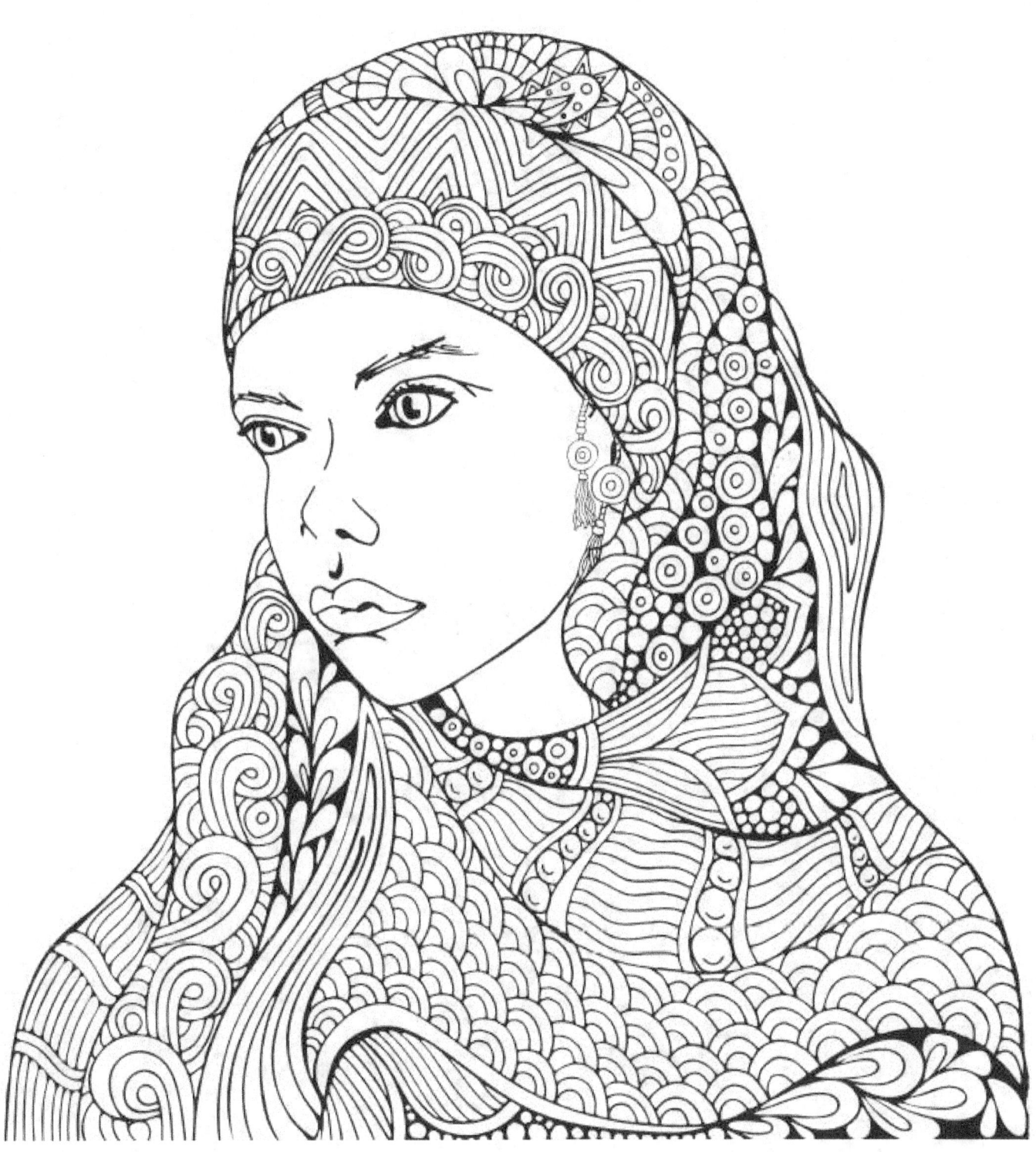

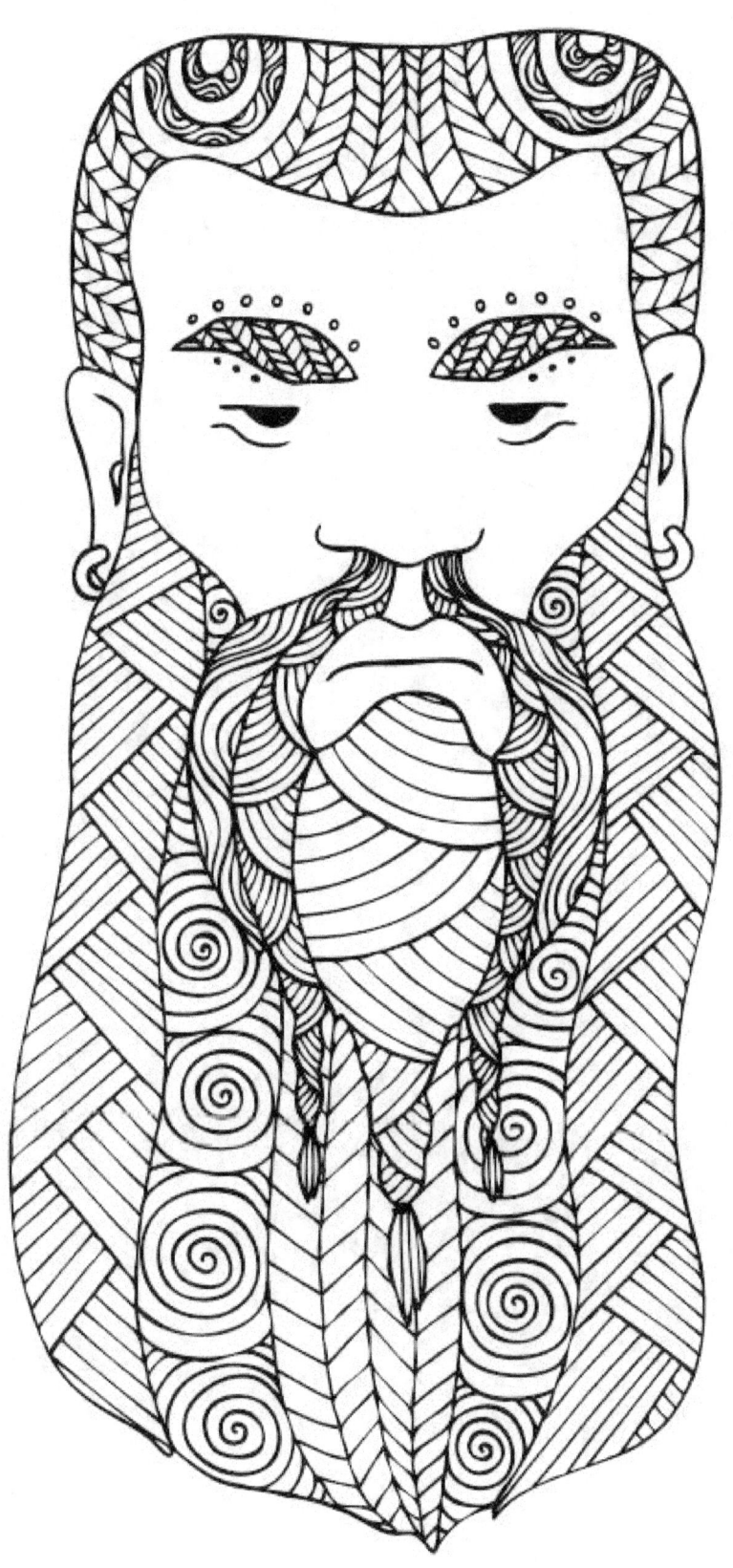

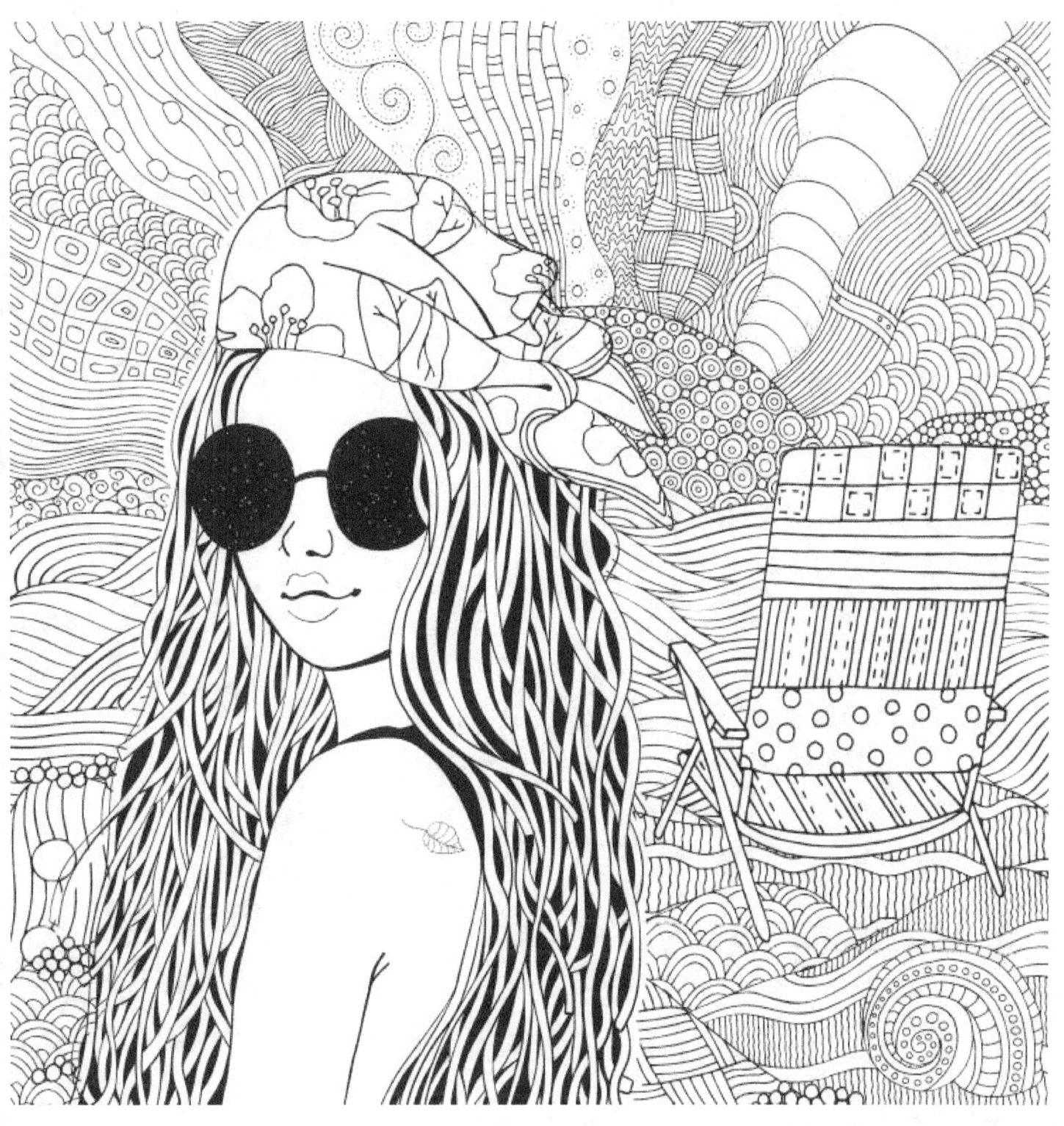

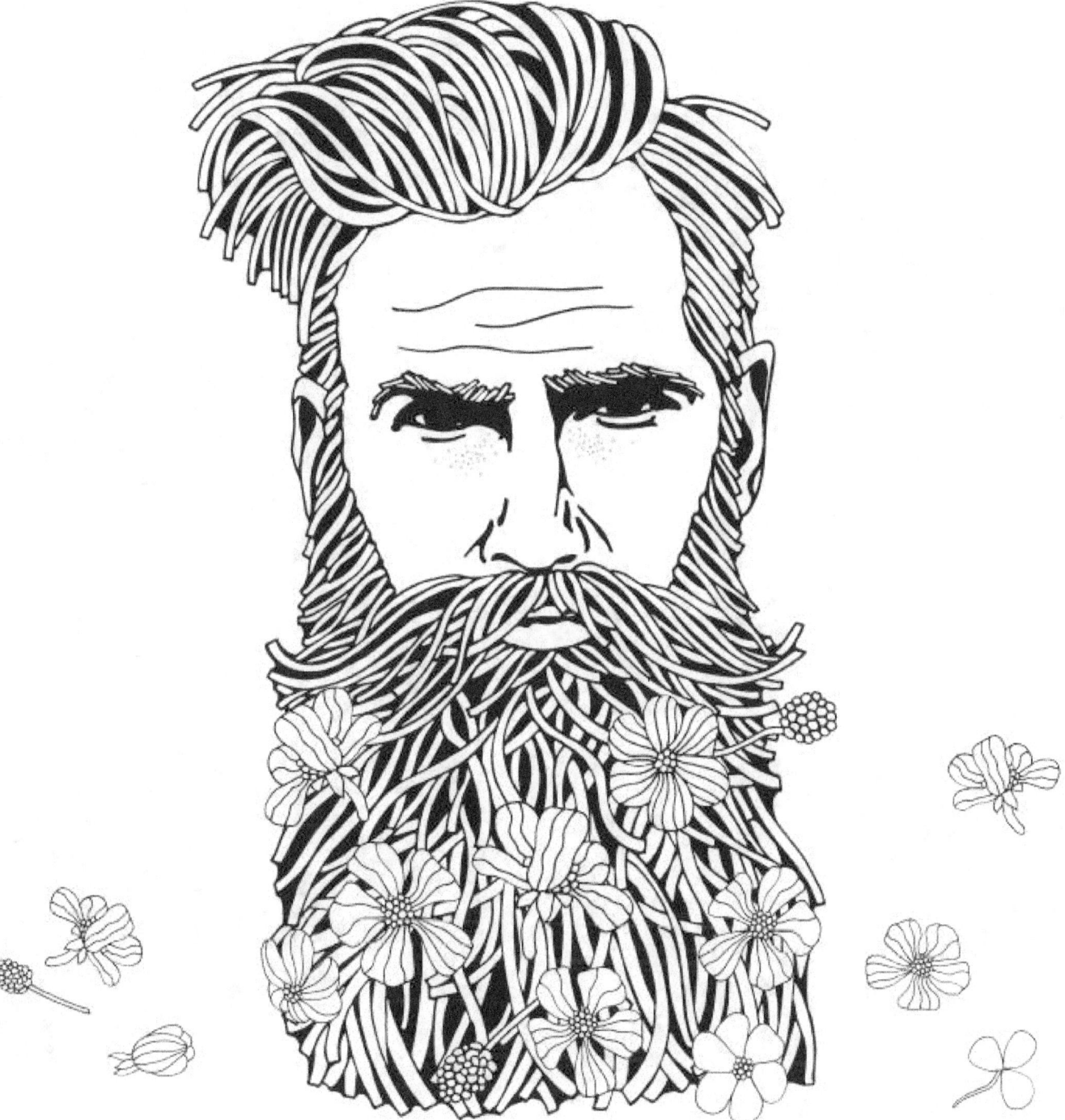

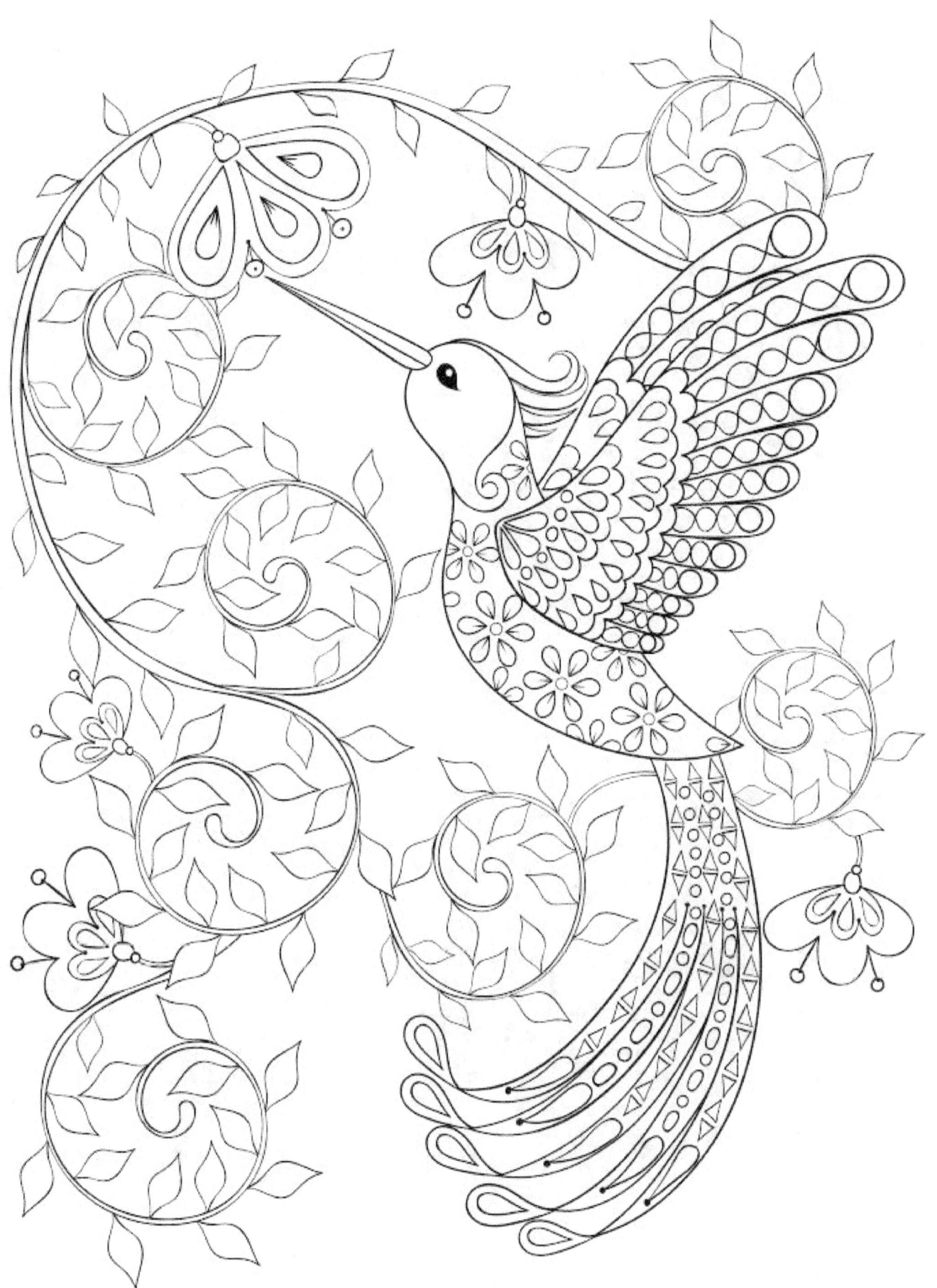

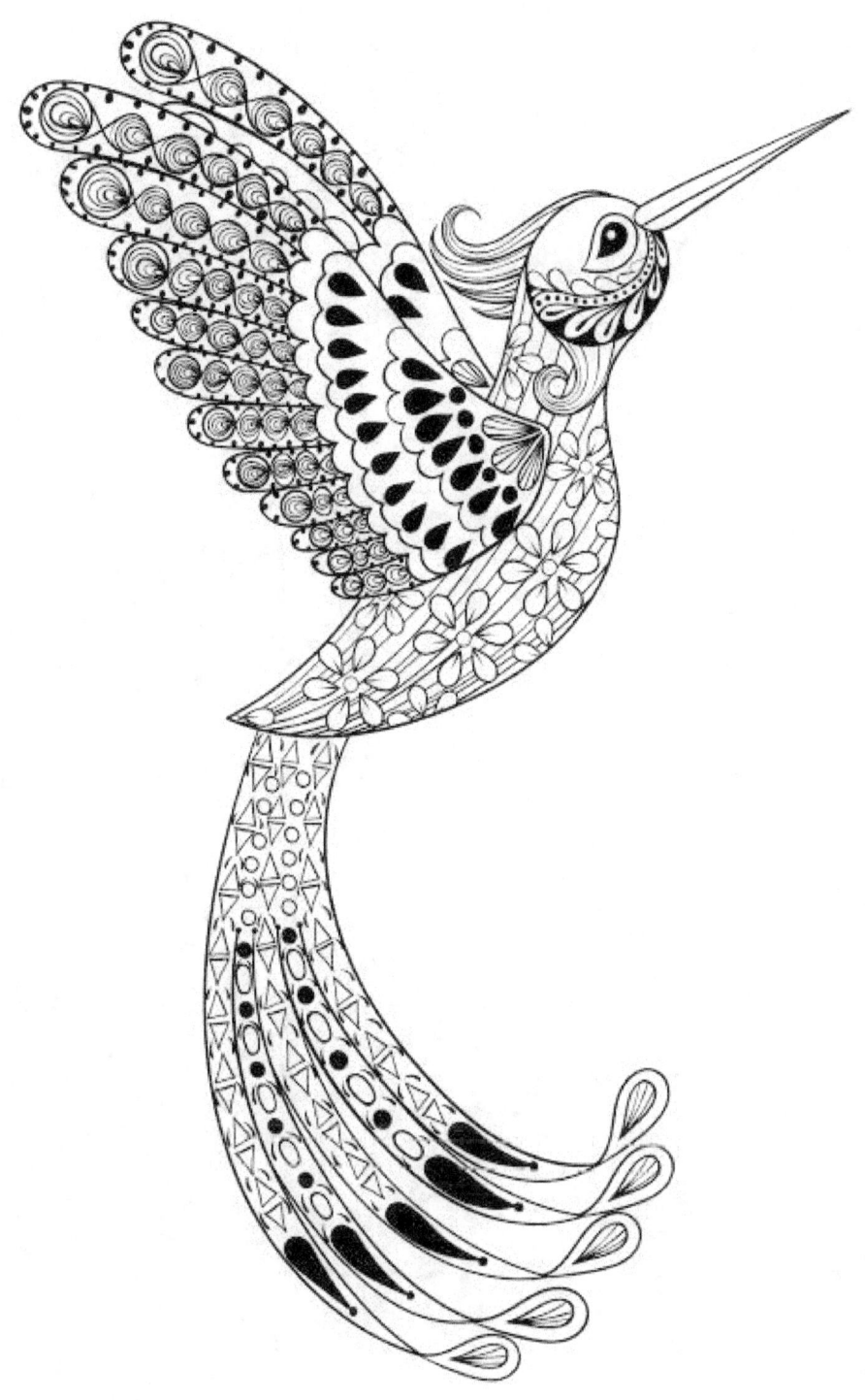

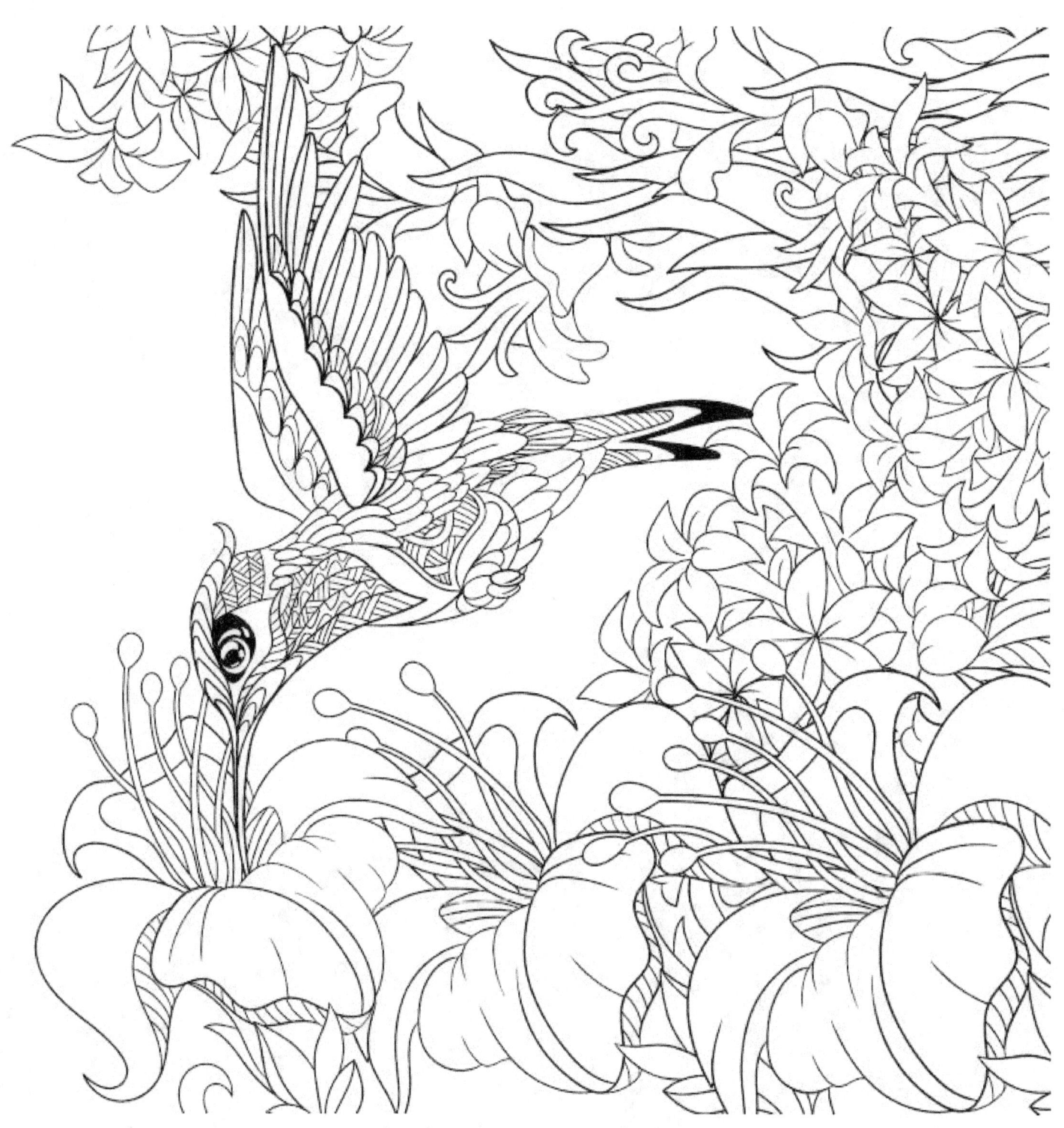

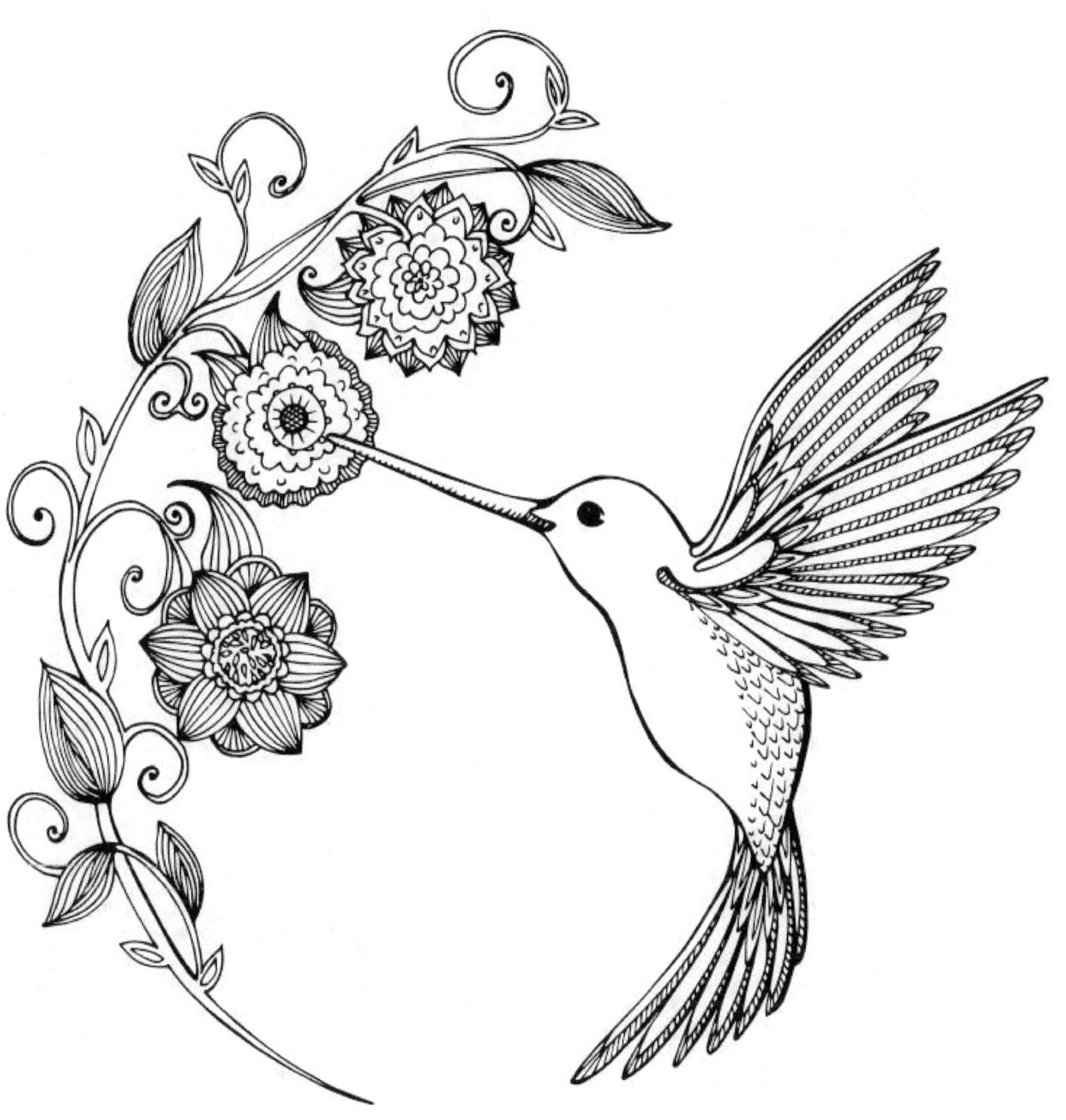

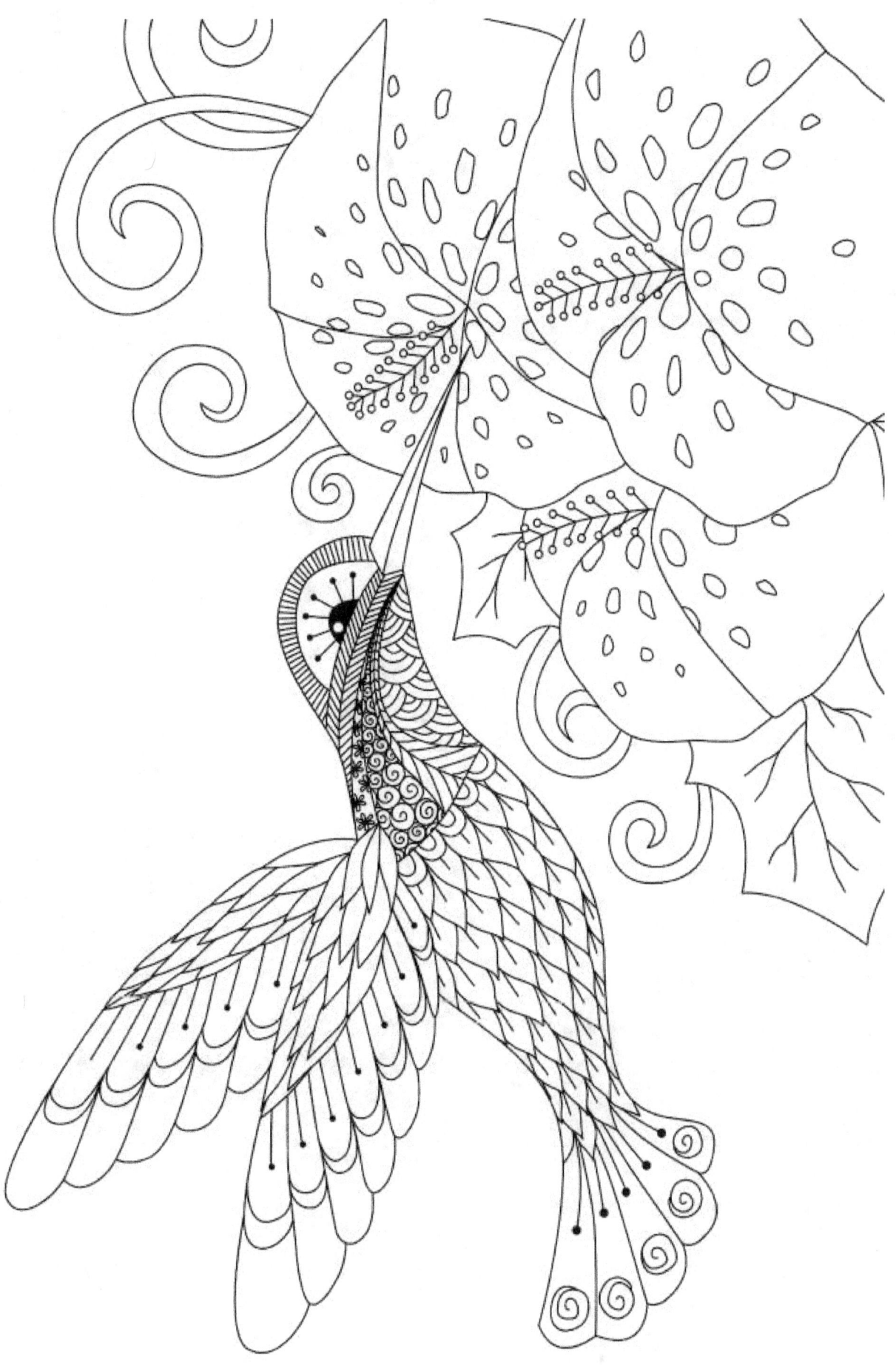

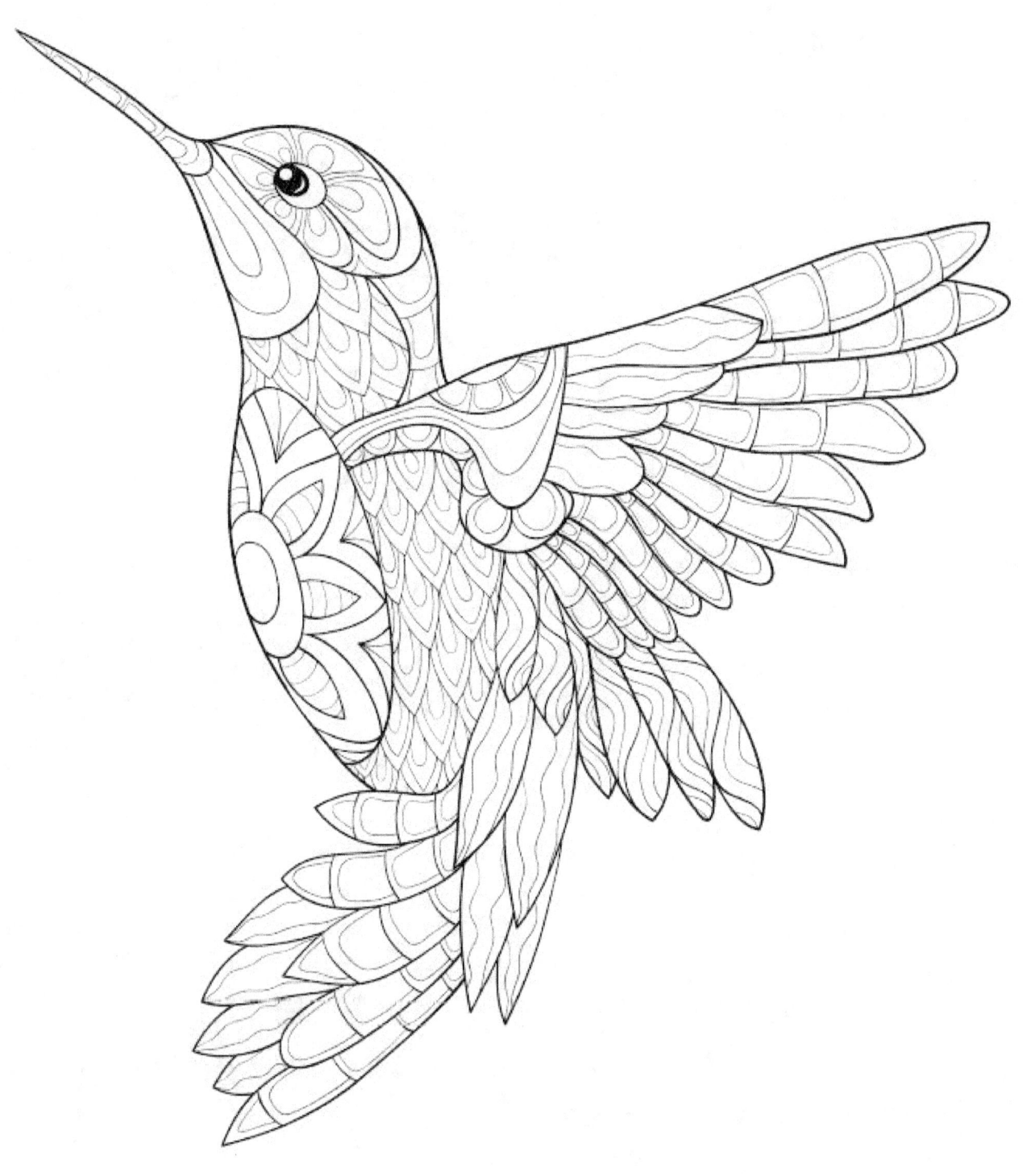

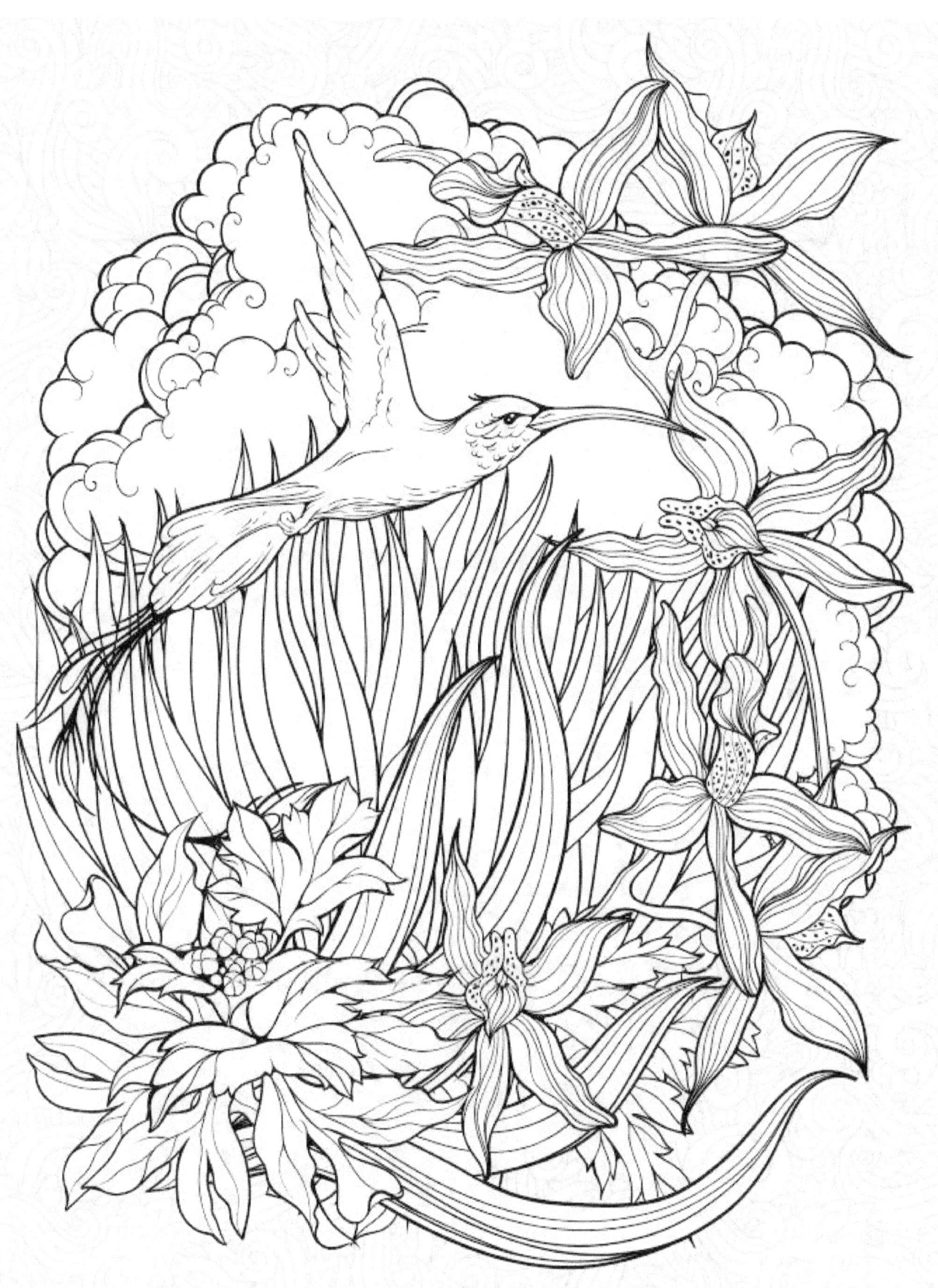

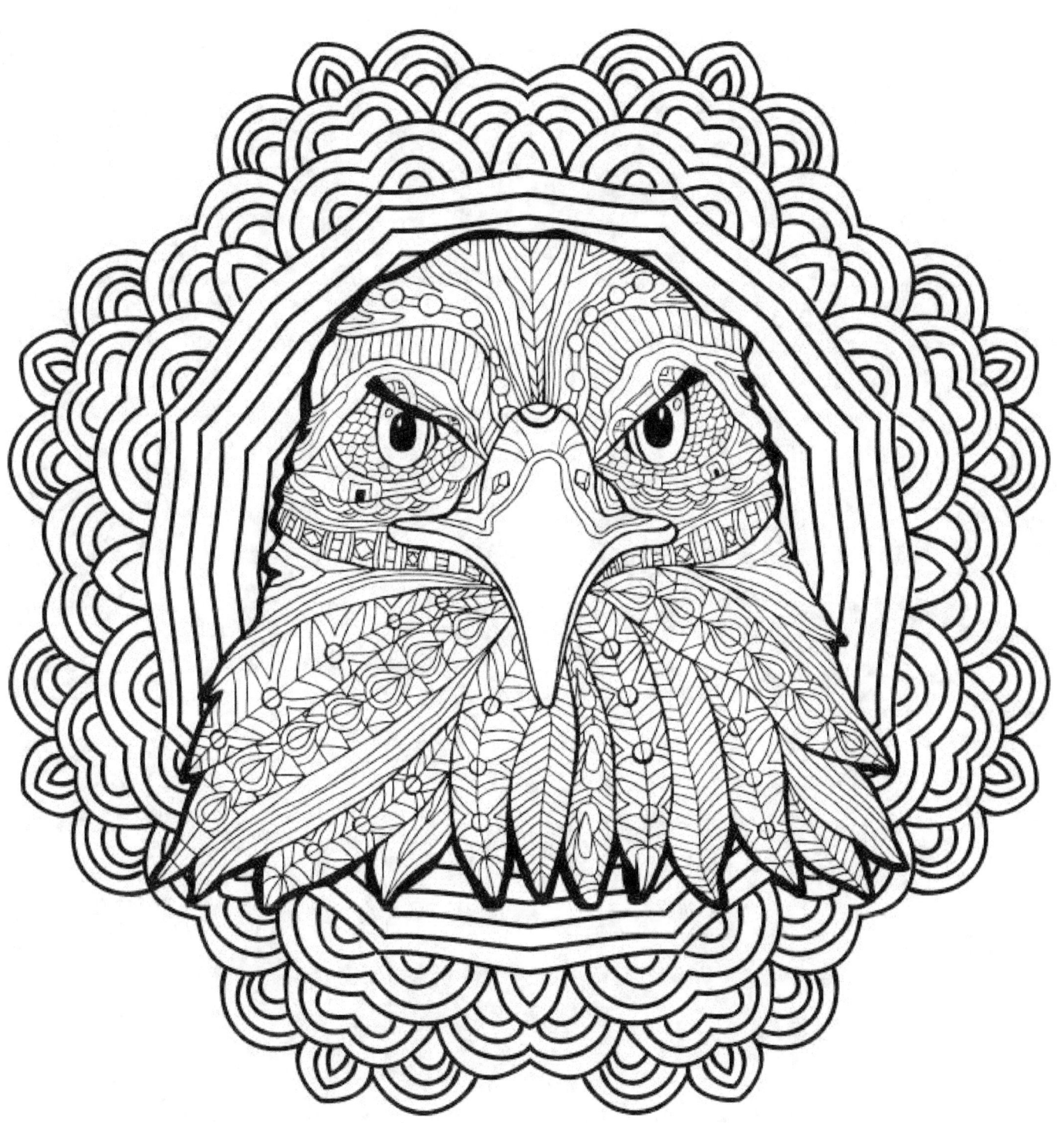

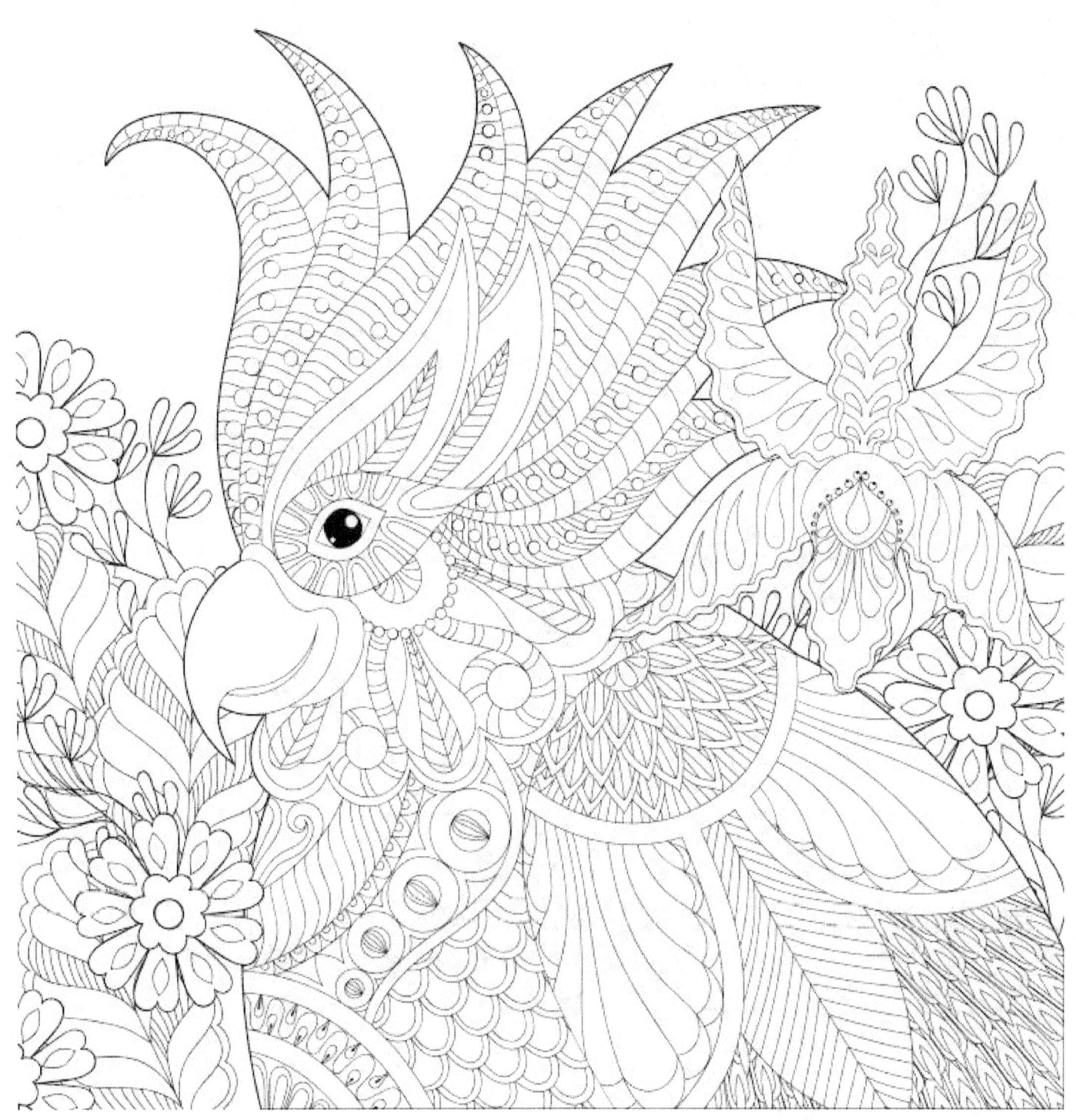

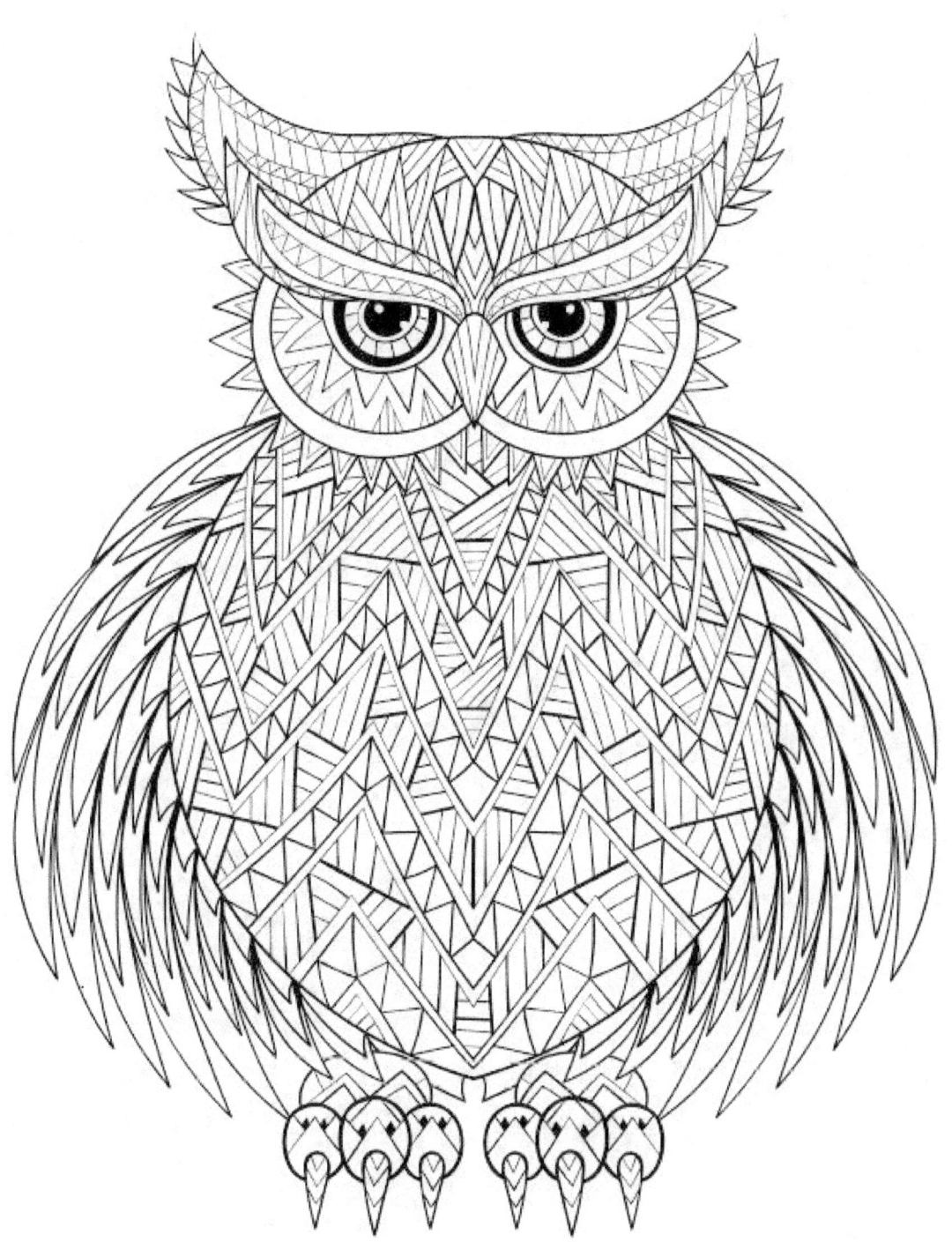

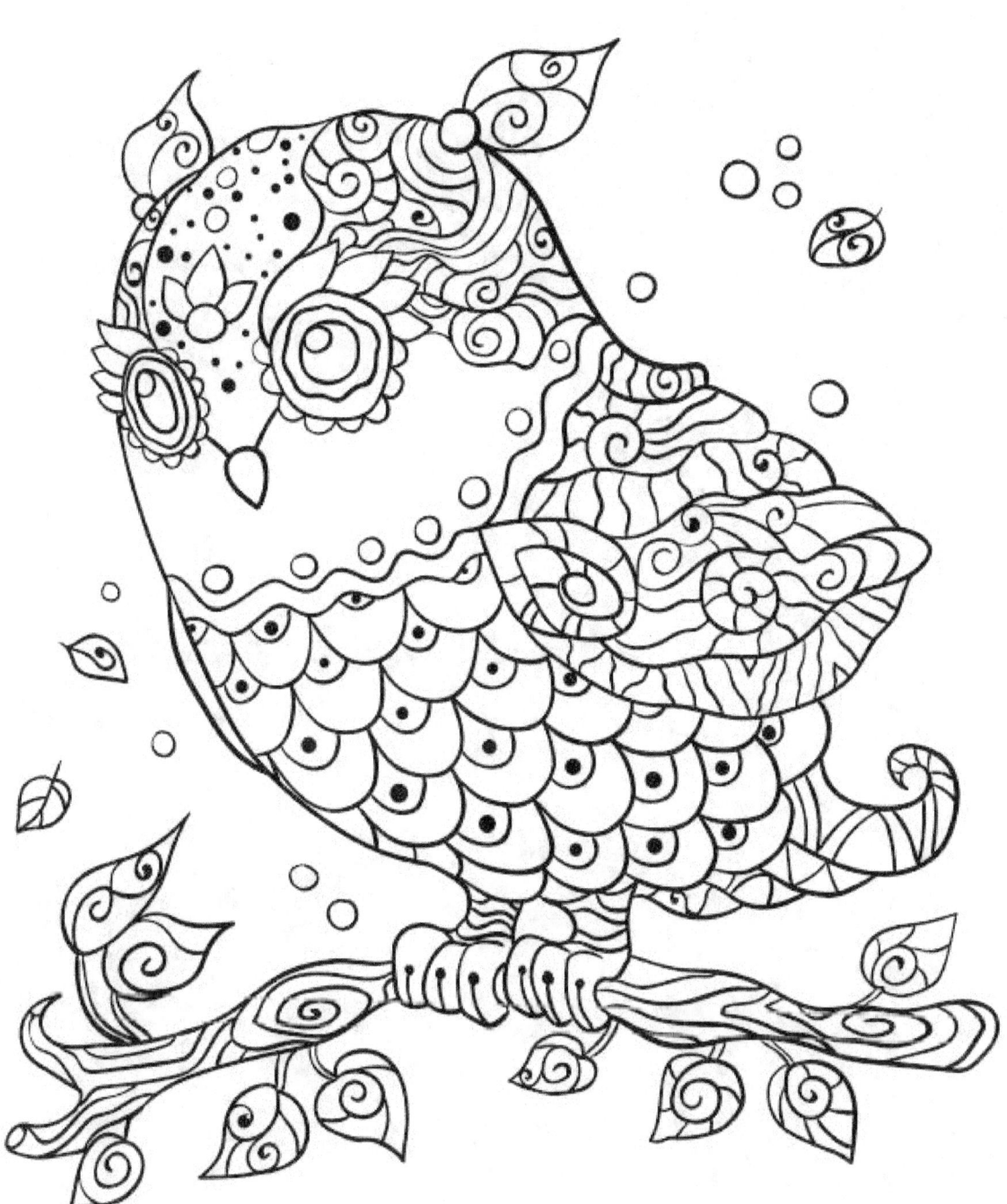

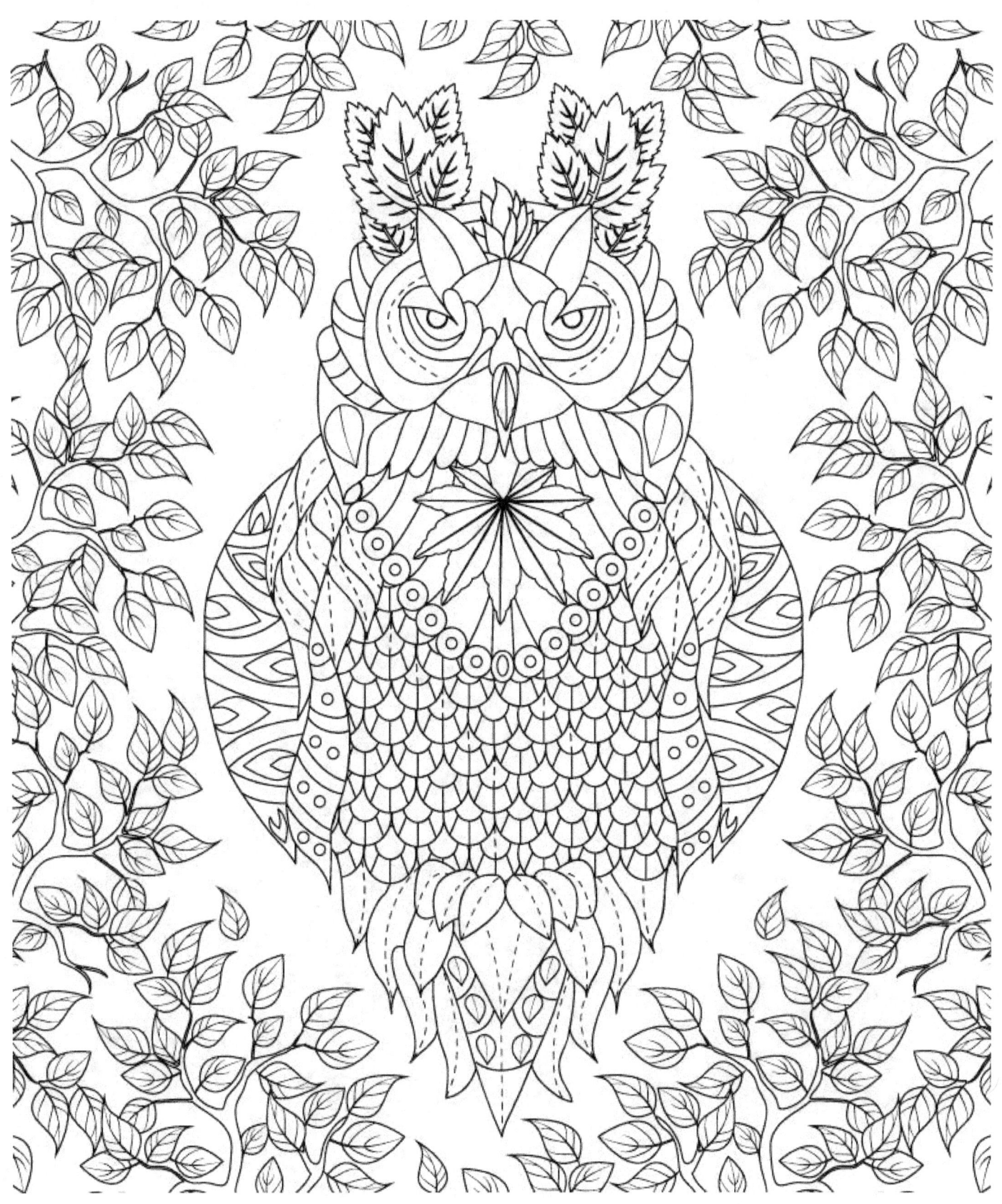

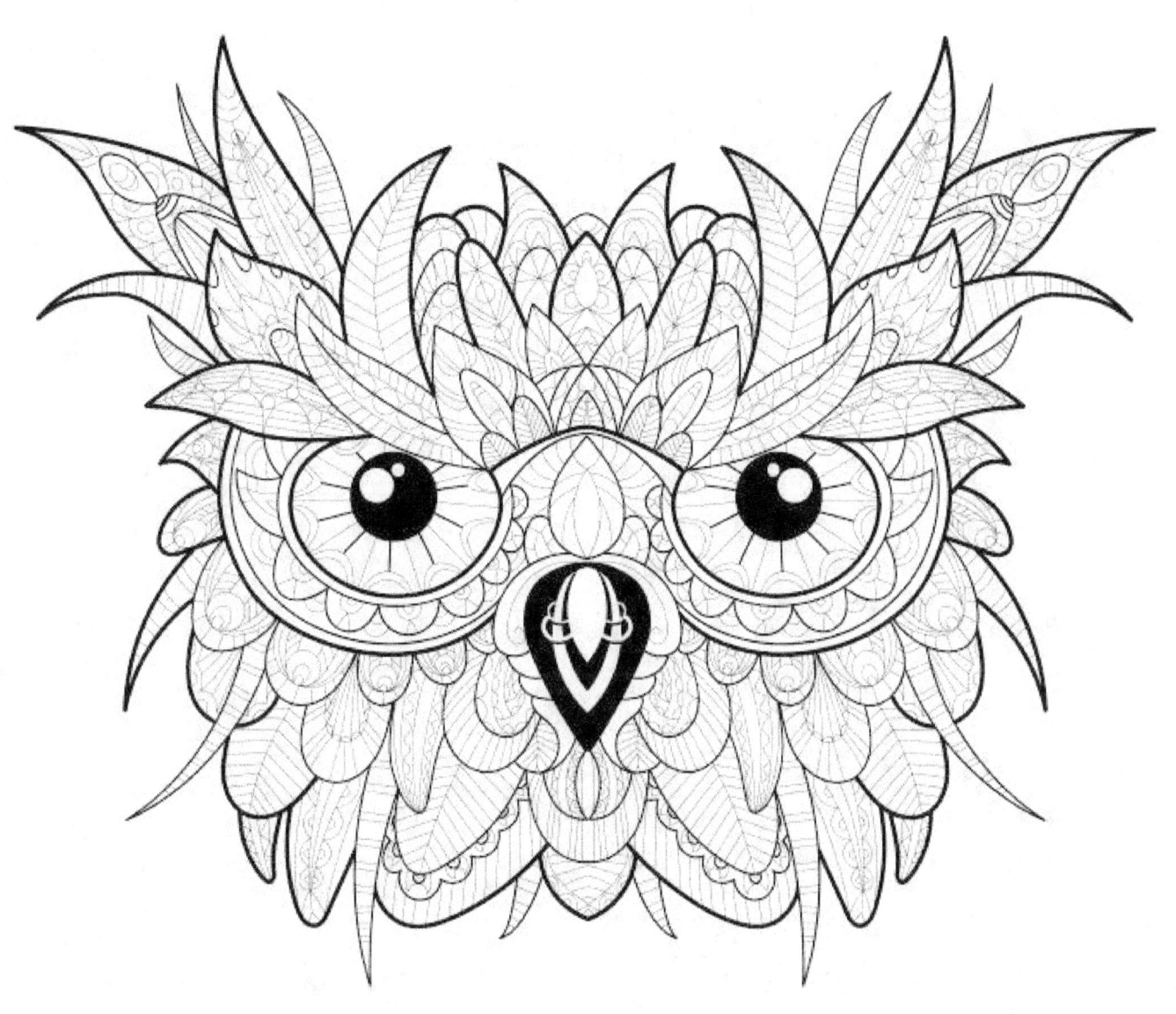

www.ingramcontent.com/pod-product-compliance
Lightning Source LLC
Chambersburg PA
CBHW081621220526
45468CB00010B/2974